The
Electoral College

by Michael Burgan

Content Adviser: Gregg Ivers, Ph.D.,
Professor, Department of Government,
American University

Reading Adviser: Rosemary Palmer, Ph.D.,
Department of Literacy, College of Education,
Boise State University

Compass Point Books ✦ Minneapolis, Minnesota

Compass Point Books
3109 West 50th Street, #115
Minneapolis, MN 55410

Visit Compass Point Books on the Internet at *www.compasspointbooks.com*
or e-mail your request to *custserv@compasspointbooks.com*

On the cover: Counting the electoral votes during the 1876 Tilden-Hayes election

Photographs ©: North Wind Picture Archives, cover, 10, 16, 17, 29, 34; Prints Old & Rare, back
cover (far left); Library of Congress, back cover, 4, 20, 21, 33; Joseph Sohm/ChromoSohm
Inc./Corbis, 5; Bruce Weaver/AFP/Getty Images, 6; Schwarz Shaul/Corbis Sygma, 7; The
Granger Collection, New York, 9, 12; Jason Maehl/BigStockPhoto, 11; National Portrait Gallery,
Smithsonian Institution/Art Resource, N.Y., 13, 30, 31; Victorian Traditions/Shutterstock, 15; Stock
Montage/Getty Images, 19; PhotoSpin, 22; Private Collection/Peter Newark American Pictures/The
Bridgeman Art Library, 23, 25; Collection of the New York Historical Society/The Bridgeman Art
Library, 26; NARA, 27; Kean Collection/Getty Images, 28; Bettmann/Corbis, 35; Jonathan Larsen/
BigStockPhoto, 36; Scott Olson/Getty Images, 38; Jimmy Margulies, *The New Jersey Record*, used
by permission, 40.

Editor: Anthony Wacholtz
Page Production: Blue Tricycle
Photo Researcher: Eric Gohl
Cartographer: XNR Productions, Inc.
Library Consultant: Kathleen Baxter

Creative Director: Keith Griffin
Editorial Director: Carol Jones
Managing Editor: Catherine Neitge

Library of Congress Cataloging-in-Publication Data
Burgan, Michael.
 The Electoral college / by Michael Burgan.
   p. cm. — (We the people)
 Includes bibliographical references and index.
 ISBN-13: 978-0-7565-2455-5 (library binding)
 ISBN-10: 0-7565-2455-5 (library binding)
 ISBN-13: 978-0-7565-3213-0 (paperback)
 ISBN-10: 0-7565-3213-2 (paperback)
1. Electoral college—United States—History—Juvenile literature. 2. Presidents—United States—
Election—Juvenile literature. I. Title. II. Series.
 JK529.B875 2007
  324.6'3—dc22   2006027088

TABLE OF CONTENTS

A VOTE TO REMEMBER

On November 7, 2000, more than 100 million Americans voted for a new U.S. president. The two candidates were Vice President Al Gore and George W. Bush, the governor of Texas. When all the votes were counted, Gore had almost 540,000 more than Bush. Yet, Bush was sworn in as the 43rd president of the United States. What caused Gore to lose the election?

George W. Bush was sworn in as president on January 20, 2001.

Democratic candidate Al Gore (left) and his running mate, Joseph Lieberman

Gore had received more popular votes than Bush. These votes are cast by citizens in voting booths across the nation. But under the U.S. Constitution, the president is chosen by people who form what is called the Electoral College. This "college" is not a building, and the group that forms it does not exist all the time. Its specially chosen electors meet in each state every four years to vote for a

5

president. The results of the popular vote in each state decide who will win that state's electoral votes. When the electoral votes are tallied, a candidate must receive at least 270 to become president.

After election night 2000, there was still no president-elect. Vice President Gore had won 255 electoral votes, while Governor Bush had 246. Whoever won Florida's 25

OFFICIAL BALLOT, GENERAL ELECTION
PALM BEACH COUNTY, FLORIDA
NOVEMBER 7, 2000

OFFICIAL BALLOT, GENERAL ELECTION
PALM BEACH COUNTY, FLORIDA
NOVEMBER 7, 2000

ELECTORS
FOR PRESIDENT
AND
VICE PRESIDENT

te for the candidates will
be a vote for their electors.)

(Vote for Group)

(REPUBLICAN)
GEORGE W. BUSH · PRESIDENT   3
DICK CHENEY · VICE PRESIDENT

(DEMOCRATIC)
AL GORE · PRESIDENT   5
JOE LIEBERMAN · VICE PRESIDENT

(LIBERTARIAN)
HARRY BROWNE · PRESIDENT   7
ART OLIVIER · VICE PRESIDENT

(GREEN)
RALPH NADER · PRESIDENT   9
WINONA LaDUKE · VICE PRESIDENT

(SOCIALIST WORKERS)
JAMES HARRIS · PRESIDENT   11
MARGARET TROWE · VICE PRESIDENT

(NATURAL LAW)
JOHN HAGELIN · PRESIDENT   13
NAT GOLDHABER · VICE PRESIDENT

4   (REFORM)
       PAT BUCHANAN · PRESIDENT
       EZOLA FOSTER · VICE PRESIDENT

6   (SOCIALIST)
       DAVID McREYNOLDS · PRESIDENT
       MARY CAL HOLLIS · VICE PRESIDENT

8   (CONSTITUTION)
       HOWARD PHILLIPS · PRESIDENT
       J. CURTIS FRAZIER · VICE PRESIDENT

10   (WORKERS WORLD)
       MONICA MOOREHEAD · PRESIDENT
       GLORIA La RIVA · VICE PRESIDENT

WRITE-IN CANDIDATE
To vote for a write-in candidate, follow the
directions on the long stub of your ballot card.

The layout of the Palm Beach County ballot confused some voters.

electoral votes would become the new president. Although Bush seemed to have won more popular votes there, the count was very close, and the voting had not gone smoothly. Some voters had not understood the ballots they used to cast their votes. Some ballots were rejected by the machines designed to read them.

In the weeks after the election, Gore and Bush fought a long legal battle. Gore argued that the votes in some Florida counties should be recounted by hand. Bush said that Florida courts had made a mistake when they said

Protesters gathered at the Florida State Supreme Court where the recounts took place.

these manual recounts could go on. The case finally reached the U.S. Supreme Court, the most powerful court

7

in the country. The court ruled that the recount had to stop. Bush had more popular votes than Gore in Florida, giving him the state's 25 electoral votes. With his victory in Florida, Bush had 271 electoral votes—just enough to become president.

The result of the election angered some of Gore's supporters. They believed Gore could have won the recount in Florida. Other Americans wondered why the winner of the popular vote did not become president. The problems in Florida put a spotlight on the role of the Electoral College in the U.S. government.

The 2000 election stirred up an old debate. Some Americans wanted to end the Electoral College and just use the popular vote. Others said that the writers of the U.S. Constitution had good reasons for creating the college, and it should remain in place. Still other Americans said the college should remain in place, but the way each state awards its electoral votes should be changed. The debate continues today.

8

CREATING A NEW GOVERNMENT

The roots of the Electoral College go back more than 200 years. The United States had won its independence from Great Britain, and its government was based on the Articles of Confederation. Under the Articles, the states acted almost like separate nations. They could print their own money and sometimes argued with each other over trade. The national government lacked the power to end these arguments or to force the states to pay taxes.

In 1787, delegates from all of the 13 states except Rhode

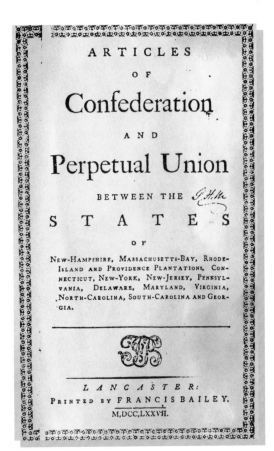

The Articles of Confederation were printed in 1777.

Island were sent to Philadelphia to strengthen the existing national government. Instead, after more than three months of debate, they created a new one. This system of government is detailed in the U.S. Constitution, and the Philadelphia meeting is known as the Constitutional Convention.

George Washington presided over the Constitutional Convention.

The U.S. Supreme Court has the highest authority in the judicial system.

The delegates at the convention created a federal system. This meant the power to rule would be shared by the states and the national government. The delegates also wanted to balance the power within the national government, so they created three distinct branches—legislative, executive, and judicial. The legislative branch makes laws for the country, the executive branch carries out the laws, and the judicial branch has courts that make sure the laws are carried out fairly.

CHOOSING THE EXECUTIVE

The Constitutional Convention delegates had various ideas on who would lead the executive branch. Most delegates wanted a single person in charge, but Edmund Randolph of Virginia thought three people should share the position. The delegates debated how many people should head the executive branch, then decided on one. A single executive worked fine on the state level, and it was what people were used to. Once the delegates agreed on having one executive leader—who

Edmund Rudolph (1753–1813)

12

came to be called the president—they debated how this person would be chosen. Most states favored having the legislative branch choose the executive. The legislative branch is now called Congress, and it consists of the House of Representatives and the Senate.

Some delegates, however, called for a direct election of the president. The candidate who received the most popular votes across the country would take the position. Some people feared that if a direct election was not used, national lawmakers would work in secret to choose an executive. "If the people should elect," Gouverneur Morris of New

Gouverneur Morris (1752–1816)

Jersey said, "they will never fail to prefer some man of distinguished character."

Not all the delegates shared Morris' faith that the people would always choose men of good character. At the time, most of the delegates assumed George Washington would be the first president. He became a national hero as commander in chief of the U.S. military during the American Revolution. Other political leaders were not well-known outside of their home states. Americans did not have television, radio, or the Internet to provide them with news. Even newspapers were not common everywhere, and news traveled slowly. Delegates wondered if voters could learn enough about presidential candidates to choose one wisely.

Other delegates feared that the largest states would control the process for selecting presidents. Leaders in a state such as Pennsylvania or Massachusetts could support a local candidate. Then the state's large pool of voters could help that candidate win.

Some Southerners had another reason for opposing

George Washington's military and leadership experience made him the prime candidate for the presidency.

direct elections. The number of representatives each state would send to the House of Representatives was to be based on its population. A census would be taken to count the

The slave population was important to Southern states in the electoral-vote system.

people in each state. The decision was made that every five slaves would be counted as three people in the census. Slaves were most common in the South, and their presence helped boost the number of Southern representatives in Congress. Therefore, Southern delegates preferred using Congress to choose a president so the South would have more influence in the process. Since slaves could not vote, they would have no influence in a direct election.

THE ELECTORAL COLLEGE

Since the delegates could not agree on the process of electing a president, a new system was needed. Some delegates suggested using people called electors from each state who would discuss which of the candidates would make the best president. Then they would vote, and the votes would be counted.

By August 31, the delegates still could not reach an agreement. James Wilson of Pennsylvania later described how hard it was for the delegates to

James Wilson (1742–1798)

17

decide how to choose an executive. He said, "The subject of presidential selection … is in truth the most difficult of all on which we have had to decide."

Finally, on September 4, a special committee proposed how an electoral-vote system could work. The delegates debated some more before accepting this system. Some historians today suggest that the delegates were not truly happy with the system they created. But after months of debate, they wanted to finish the Constitution. The electoral-vote system seemed the best compromise for choosing an executive. Alexander Hamilton, one of the delegates, said about the Electoral College: "If the manner of it be not per-fect, it is at least excellent."

The process for choosing the president is outlined in Article II, Section 1 of the Constitution. Each state's num-ber of electors is based on the number of people it sends to Congress. Since each state has two senators and at least one House representative, each state has at least three electoral votes. No member of Congress or other government official

The Constitution was created at Independence Hall in Philadelphia.

can serve as an elector.

The delegates decided that each state legislature would determine how its electors were chosen. Some decided to use a popular vote, while others directed lawmakers to choose them. After the electors were chosen, they would meet to cast their votes.

Each elector voted for two candidates. At least one of them had to be from a state other than the elector's home

The House of Representatives chose the president if the voting resulted in a tie.

state. The person who received a majority of the votes—half of the total number of votes plus one—became president. The person who came in second became vice president. Since it was likely that more than two candidates would run for the presidency, it was possible that no candidate would receive a majority of the votes. In this case, the House of Representatives would choose the president from the five candidates with the most votes. The House would also break a tie vote.

PARTIES AND ELECTORAL VOTES

People with similar views often joined together to form political parties. They helped each other win elections, and the winning candidate often gave jobs to the party's members. Alexander Hamilton and other writers of the Constitution disliked political parties. They thought parties with opposing beliefs created hatred within a country. They thought everyone should work for

Alexander Hamilton (1755–1804)

21

the common good, and personal interests should be pushed aside. Still, the differences in opinion caused the men to create two political parties—the Federalists and the Anti-Federalists.

People who supported the new government were called Federalists. Those who thought the Constitution took too much power from the states were called Anti-Federalists. During the 1790s, these two groups formed the nation's first political parties.

While George Washington served

The Constitution was written to detail the structure of the U.S. government.

as president, members of the two groups set aside their differences for the most part. In 1797, Washington left the presidency, and John Adams—a Federalist—became president. Thomas Jefferson—the leader of the Anti-Federalists, or Democratic Republicans—served as Adams' vice president. Jefferson and Adams had both run for president, and Jefferson came in second. Because of the structure of the Electoral College, two men from different parties served together as president and vice president.

John Adams (1735–1826)

With the 1796 election, state political leaders supported electors who would vote for their party's candidate. They did

23

not want the electors to act on their own. The writers of the Constitution, however, had hoped the electors would be independent. They also hoped the electors would just narrow down the number of candidates and not favor one candidate. Then Congress would make the final selection in the House of Representatives. But the growth of political parties changed that. Party leaders, not the electors, narrowed down the number of candidates. Today, each party selects just one candidate to run for president. However, only a few parties are large enough to gain enough support across the country.

Despite what the writers of the Constitution intended, Congress has chosen a president just two times since 1789. The first was the election of 1800.

A TIE LEADS TO CHANGE

The election of 1800 again featured Thomas Jefferson against John Adams. Before the election, political leaders in some states changed how their states chose electors in order to help their candidate. Massachusetts had used a direct election, letting the public vote for the electors. But the Federalists, who controlled the state legislature, wanted to make sure Adams got the state's votes. So lawmakers switched the process, giving themselves the power to choose electors.

In Virginia, Democratic Republicans controlled the state legislature. Previously, voters

Thomas Jefferson (1743–1826)

25

chose electors by district. The Federalists were strong in certain districts and had a chance to vote in some of the electors. In response, the Democratic Republicans changed the system so Virginia's electors were chosen by direct election across the state, not by district. Overall, Virginia had more Democratic Republican supporters than Federalists. The switch meant electors who favored Jefferson would be more likely to win.

When the electoral votes were cast, Jefferson tied with Aaron Burr. Jefferson and Burr were both Democratic Republicans. One of the party's electors was supposed to withhold a vote for Burr, since Jefferson was the party's choice for president. When the elector mistakenly failed to do so, the

Aaron Burr (1756–1836)

two men tied.

According to the U.S. Constitution, the House of Representatives was responsible for breaking the tie. The members of the House voted for the president by state. Since there were 16 states at this time, either Burr or Jefferson would need the votes from nine states to become president. Voting went on for several weeks before Jefferson finally won.

	Thomas Jefferson of Virginia	Aaron Burr of New York	John Adams of Massachusetts	Charles Pinckney of South Carolina	John Jay of New York
New Hampshire			6	6	
Massachusetts			16	16	
Rhode Island			4	3	1
Connecticut			9	9	
Vermont			4	4	
New York	12	12			
New Jersey			7	7	
Pennsylvania	8	8	7	7	
Delaware			3	3	
Maryland	5	5	5	5	
Virginia	21	21			
Kentucky	4	4			
North Carolina	8	8	4	4	
Tennessee	3	3			
South Carolina	8	8			
Georgia	4	4			
	73	73	65	64	1

Thomas Jefferson and Aaron Burr each received 73 votes in the 1800 election.

Confusion over who would serve as president and vice president led to a change in the electoral system. In 1804, the 12th Amendment to the Constitution was passed. This amendment allowed electors two votes—one for president and one for vice president. If no one won a majority for president, the House of Representatives would choose the winner. Similarly, the Senate would choose the vice president. With this change, parties began to name their presidential and vice presidential candidates. From then on, the person who became vice president was often seen as his party's next presidential candidate. The vice president gained experience, and more people across the country became familiar with him.

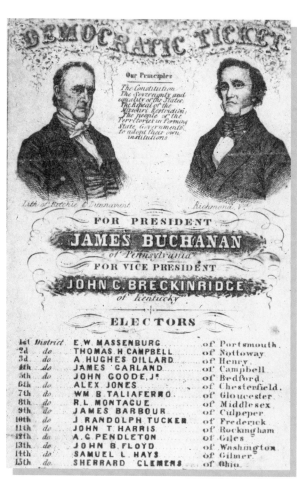

John Breckinridge served as James Buchanan's vice president before running against Abraham Lincoln the following election.

MORE NOTABLE ELECTIONS

The second election to reach the House of Representatives came in 1824. By then, the Federalists no longer existed. The Democratic Republicans were the only major party. Its leaders chose William Crawford as their top choice, but some members of the party wanted other men to run for the presidency instead. In the end, Andrew Jackson, John Quincy Adams, and Henry Clay ran against one another. Crawford became ill and was no longer considered a strong candidate.

William Crawford (1772–1834)

Henry Clay (1777–1852)

That year, Jackson won the popular vote and the most electoral votes. However, he did not receive a majority of the electoral votes. That meant the House of Representatives would choose the president. In the House, Clay told his supporters to back Adams, and with the extra support, Adams was chosen president. Adams then gave Clay an important position in the government. An angry Jackson complained that the two men had made a secret deal. He was also upset that he had won the popular vote but lost the election.

Since Jackson's defeat, three other men have won the

popular vote and not become president. Until 2000, the most controversial election was in 1876. That year, Democratic candidate Samuel Tilden seemed to have defeated Rutherford B. Hayes, a Republican. (This Republican party had formed in 1854 and was not related to Jefferson's Democratic Republicans.)

Samuel Tilden (1814–1886)

Tilden also seemed to have enough electoral votes to win. But the popular vote count was in dispute in three states— Louisiana, South Carolina, and Florida. As a result, these states had sent two sets of electoral votes to the House of Representatives. Congress had to decide whether to accept

31

the votes of the Democratic or Republican electors. If the Republican votes were taken from all three states, Hayes would win.

The Constitution did not address what to do if a state sent two sets of electoral votes to be counted. Congress decided to set up a special commission to consider which votes to accept. This Electoral Commission had 15 members: five senators, five House representatives, and five members of the U.S. Supreme Court. Eight commission members were Republicans and seven were Democrats. Since there were more Republicans than Democrats, the commission voted 8-7 in favor of Hayes for each of the three states.

Like Andrew Jackson, Tilden was angry about losing the election in Congress. He said, "Everybody knows that, after the recent election, the men who were elected by the people President and Vice President of the United States were 'counted out,' and men who were not elected were 'counted in' and seated." Tilden called for changes in how

In Washington, D.C., the Electoral Commission held a secret session by candlelight.

presidents were chosen, but the system remained the same.

The next candidate to win the popular vote and lose was Grover Cleveland in 1888. Benjamin Harrison won the larger states, including Ohio, New York, Pennsylvania, and Illinois, giving him 65 more electoral votes than Cleveland.

Benjamin Harrison's supporters cheered after he was nominated for president in 1888.

Several presidents have received less than a majority of the popular votes and still won through electoral votes. These include Abraham Lincoln in 1860, Harry S. Truman in 1948, and John F. Kennedy in 1960. Kennedy had less than 50 percent of the votes in his race against Richard Nixon, but he won 303 electoral votes to take the election.

CREATING A NEW SYSTEM?

The Kennedy victory came after Congress had repeatedly talked about getting rid of the Electoral College. Starting in the 1920s, the House and the Senate held many hearings to discuss this issue. In 1951, one former lawmaker spoke out against the college. He said that an electoral voter "represent[s] only the party that selected him" and not the "will of the people of the area by whom he is elected."

In 1969, Congress considered another call to let the public directly elect the president.

In 1933, the electors from New York gave the state's electoral votes to Franklin D. Roosevelt.

35

The vote in favor of the idea was 338-70 in the House, but the Senate chose not to vote on the matter. Ten years later, 51 senators supported an amendment to the Constitution to end the Electoral College and use a direct election. To pass in the Senate, however, an amendment needs 67 votes.

The Senate has failed to approve an amendment to end the Electoral College.

Discussions about the Electoral College heated up after 2000. By that time, almost all the states and the District of Columbia had agreed on one way to choose electors. The presidential candidate who won the popular vote within the state took all the electoral votes. This system is known as winner-take-all. Only Maine and Nebraska chose electors by both district results and statewide results. The winner of the overall state election received two electoral votes, and the winner of each district in the state also won a vote.

The supporters of the direct election method have said the current Electoral College system leads candidates to ignore voters in some states. Most candidates have focused on the states with the largest number of votes or states that showed voters were evenly split among the candidates. A candidate may not want to spend time and money meeting with voters in a state such as Rhode Island, which only has four electoral votes. Or a Democrat might ignore voters in Texas, since its voters have usually favored Republicans in recent presidential elections.

Democratic presidential candidate John Kerry visited a California high school in 2004.

Critics of the Electoral College have said that, at the least, lawmakers should change how the votes are awarded. Some have favored following the district system used in Maine and Nebraska. Others have called for dividing up the votes based on a state's popular vote. For example, a candidate who wins 70 percent of a state's popular vote would receive 70 percent of its electoral votes.

In 2006, a group of former lawmakers suggested each state pass a law that would award all of its electoral votes to the winner of the national popular vote. This effort was called National Popular Vote. Lawmakers in several states quickly supported the plan. Fred W. Thiele Jr., a New York

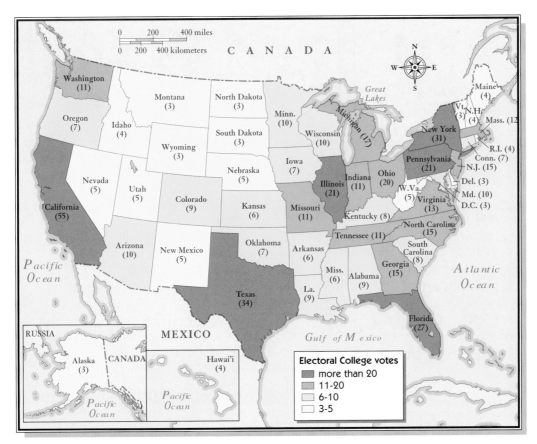

Supporters of direct election argue that candidates focus on states with the most electoral votes—like California, Texas, and New York—and ignore others.

A political cartoon depicted the Electoral College as a rundown, out-of-date car.

lawmaker, said, "The election of the President by popular vote is a goal that is supported by more than 70% of the American people. There is no rational reason in the 21st Century why the public should not be permitted to select its President by majority vote."

But the Electoral College still has its supporters. Some say the delegates at the Constitutional Convention did not want direct elections of the president. They wanted a system that chose the president at the state level. The delegates built a system designed to balance the interests of both large and small states. The candidate has to win the support of a large number of states. With a direct election, a candidate could win by taking most of the popular votes in just a few large states, even though many of the voters in the other states supported someone else.

Defenders of the Electoral College argue that the results of a direct election would not truly reflect the desire of the country as a whole. They also say that the Electoral College has not led to great problems—despite what happened in 2000 and before. Phyllis Schlafly, a conservative political writer and activist, holds this view. She wrote in 2006, "It has served us well for more than two centuries. It isn't broke and doesn't need fixing." Over time, U.S. voters, speaking through their lawmakers, will decide if they want to keep the current Electoral College or use another system to choose their president.

GLOSSARY

amendments—formal changes made to a law or legal document, such as the Constitution

ballots—paper or mechanical methods used to record votes

candidates—people running for political office

census—an official count of all the people living in a country or district

compromise—solutions that settle differences between people

constitution—a document stating the basic rules of a government

controversial—causing dispute or disagreement

delegates—people who represent a larger group of people at a meeting

district—a region within a state with a specific number of voters

electors—people who vote to choose between two or more people running for office

DID YOU KNOW?

- An elector chosen by a party who does not vote for that party's candidate is called a "faithless elector." Since 1789, there have only been 11 faithless electors.

- Since 1789, members of Congress have proposed more than 700 amendments to change the Electoral College or end it completely. The 12th Amendment is the only one that has passed.

- South Carolina was the last state to have its lawmakers choose electors. After the Civil War, it switched to popular voting.

- In 1836, neither candidate for vice president received a majority of the votes, so the election was decided by the U.S. Senate. The senators chose Richard M. Johnson of Kentucky to serve with President Martin Van Buren. No other vice president has ever been chosen by the Senate.

- The 23rd Amendment, passed in 1961, gave the District of Columbia three electoral votes, even though Washington, D.C., does not have any members of Congress.

IMPORTANT DATES

Timeline

1787 — Delegates at the Constitutional Convention create the electoral-vote system for choosing the U.S. president.

1800 — A tie in electoral votes between Thomas Jefferson and Aaron Burr leads to the House of Representatives choosing Jefferson as president.

1804 — The 12th Amendment is passed, requiring electors to cast one vote for president and one for vice president.

1824 — No candidate wins a majority of electoral votes, and the House chooses John Quincy Adams as president.

1876 — A special Electoral Commission created by Congress ends a disputed presidential election, resulting in a win for Replican Rutherford B. Hayes.

2000 — The U.S. Supreme Court ends the recount of popular votes in Florida, giving George W. Bush the state's 25 electoral votes and the presidency.

IMPORTANT PEOPLE

JOHN QUINCY ADAMS (1767–1848)

Winner of the 1824 presidential election, which was settled by the House of Representatives after no candidate won a majority of electoral votes; he was the son of former President John Adams

GEORGE W. BUSH (1946–)

Winner of the 2000 presidential election after the U.S. Supreme Court ended recounts in Florida; he is the son of former President George H.W. Bush

ALEXANDER HAMILTON (1755–1804)

Delegate at the Constitutional Convention who favored the Electoral College and later led the Federalist Party; he was killed in a duel with Aaron Burr

ANDREW JACKSON (1767–1845)

U.S. major general who won the popular vote in the 1824 presidential election but failed to win enough electoral and House of Representatives votes; he later won the presidency in 1828 and 1832

THOMAS JEFFERSON (1743–1826)

Winner of the 1800 presidential election and leader of the Democratic Republican Party; he wrote the Declaration of Independence

WANT TO KNOW MORE?

At the Library

Gottfried, Ted. *The 2000 Election.* Brookfield, Conn.: Millbrook Press, 2002.

Hewson, Martha S. *The Electoral College.* Philadelphia: Chelsea House Publishers, 2002.

Saffel, David C., ed. *The Encyclopedia of U.S. Presidential Elections.* New York: Franklin Watts, 2004.

Smalley, Carol Parenzan. *Elections & Political Parties.* Logan, Iowa: Perfection Learning, 2005.

Weidner, Daniel W. *Creating the Constitution: The People and Events that Formed the Nation.* Berkeley Heights, N.J.: Enslow, 2002.

On the Web

For more information on this topic, use FactHound.

1. Go to *www.facthound.com*

2. Type in this book ID: 0756524555

3. Click on the *Fetch It* button.

FactHound will find the best Web sites for you.

On the Road

Independence Hall

Independence Hall Visitor Center

Sixth and Market Street

Philadelphia, PA 19106

215/965-2305

Place where the Constitution was
debated and written in 1787

National Archives and Records Administration

700 Pennsylvania Ave.

Washington, D.C. 20408

866/325-7208

Archive that holds valuable documents, including the Constitution, Bill of Rights, and Declaration of Independence

Look for more We the People books about this era:

A complete list of We the People titles is available on our Web site:
www.compasspointbooks.com

INDEX

About the Author

Michael Burgan is a freelance writer of books for children and adults. A history graduate of the University of Connecticut, he has written more than 100 fiction and nonfiction children's books. For adult audiences, he has written news articles, essays, and plays. Michael Burgan is a recipient of an Educational Press Association of America award.